How to Draw Funny Monsters

by Jerry Jones

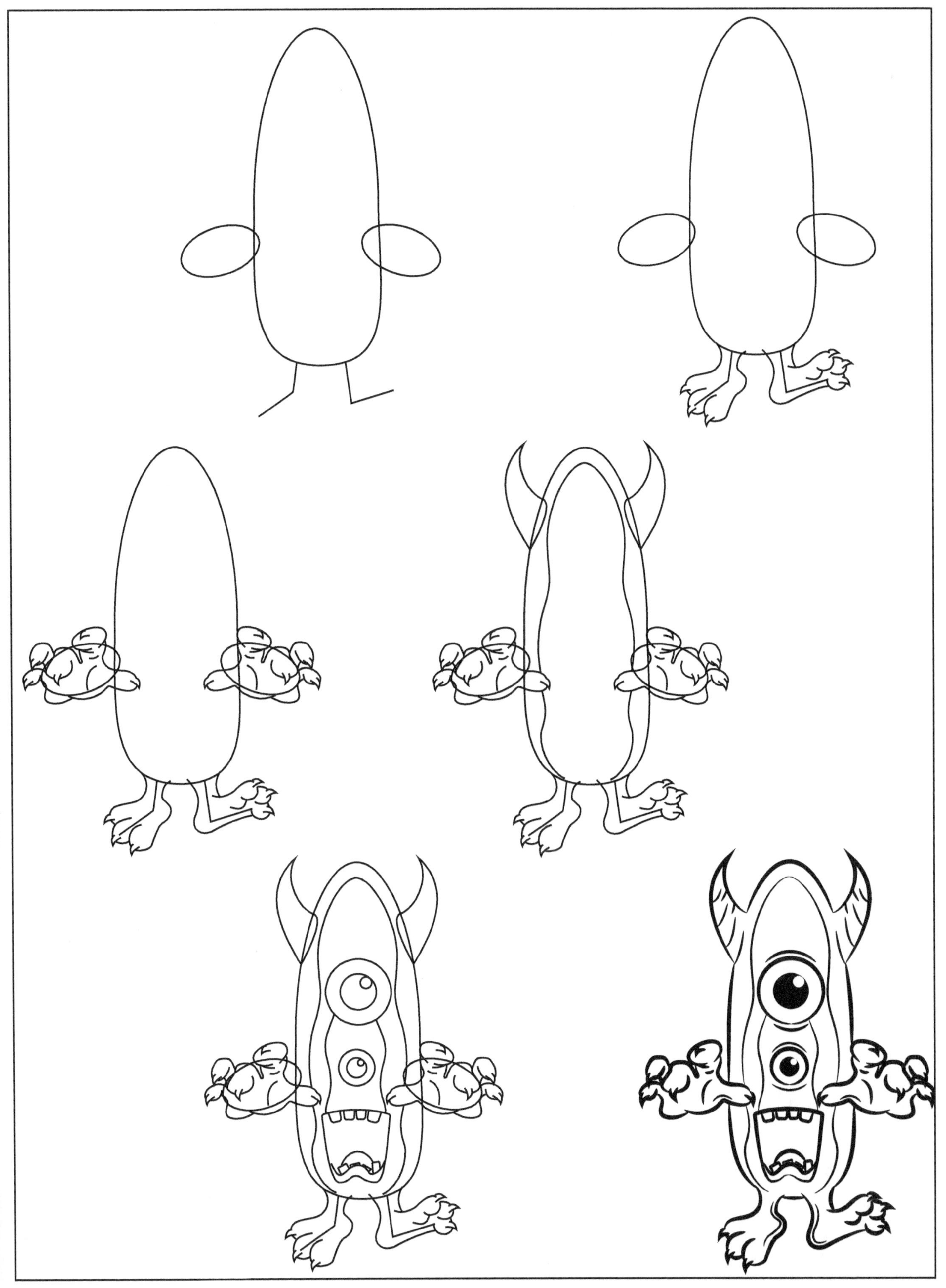

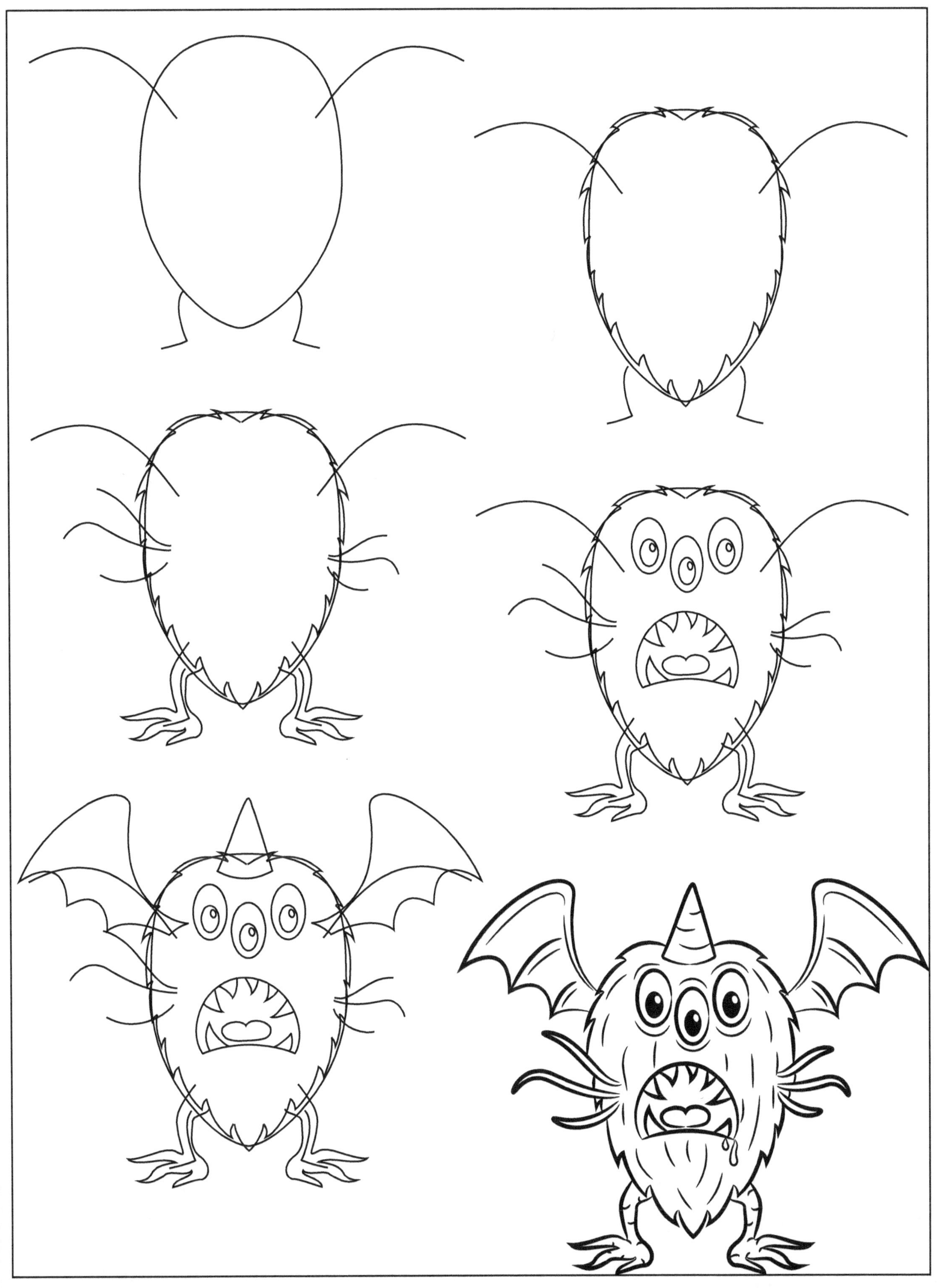

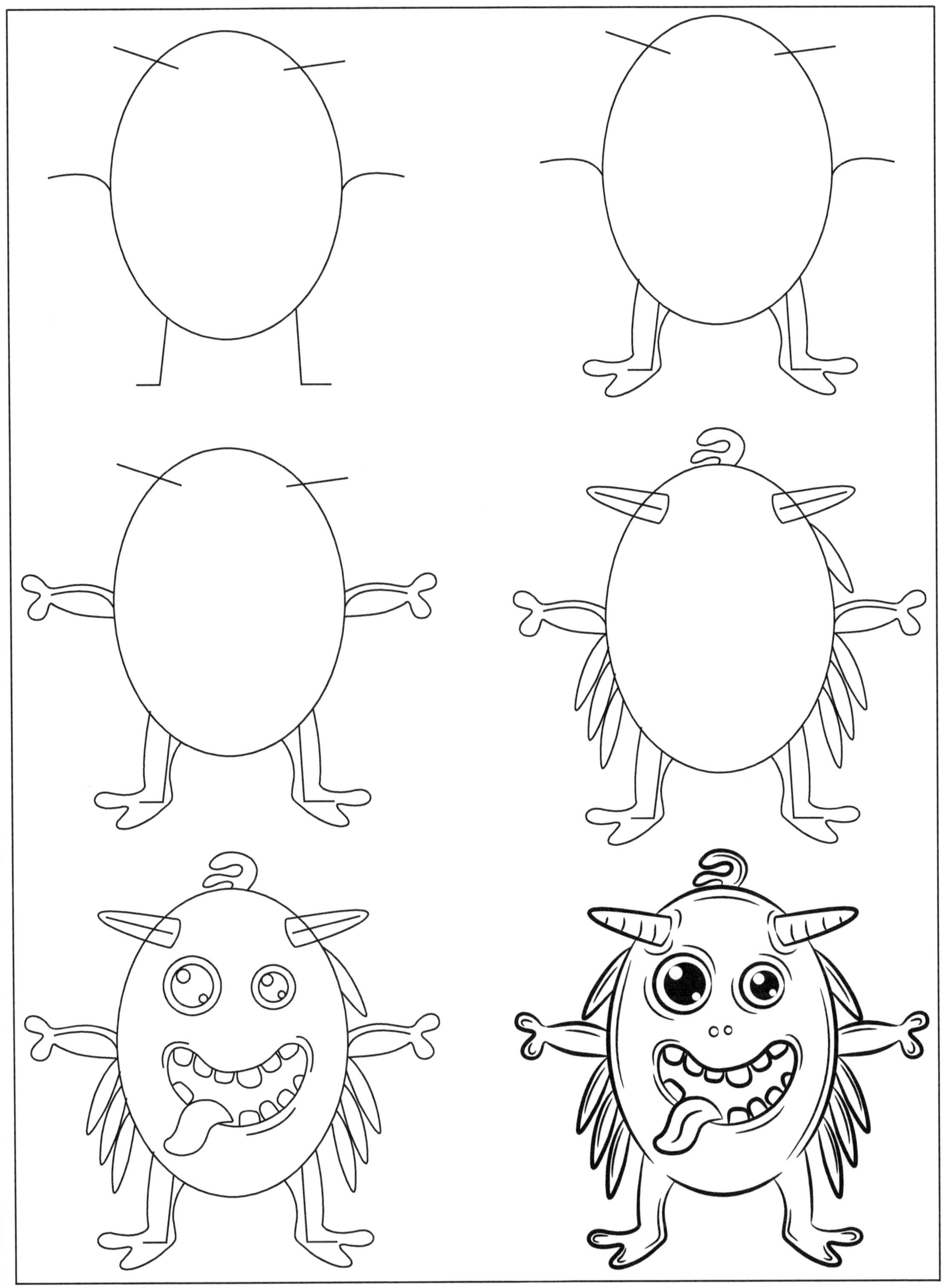

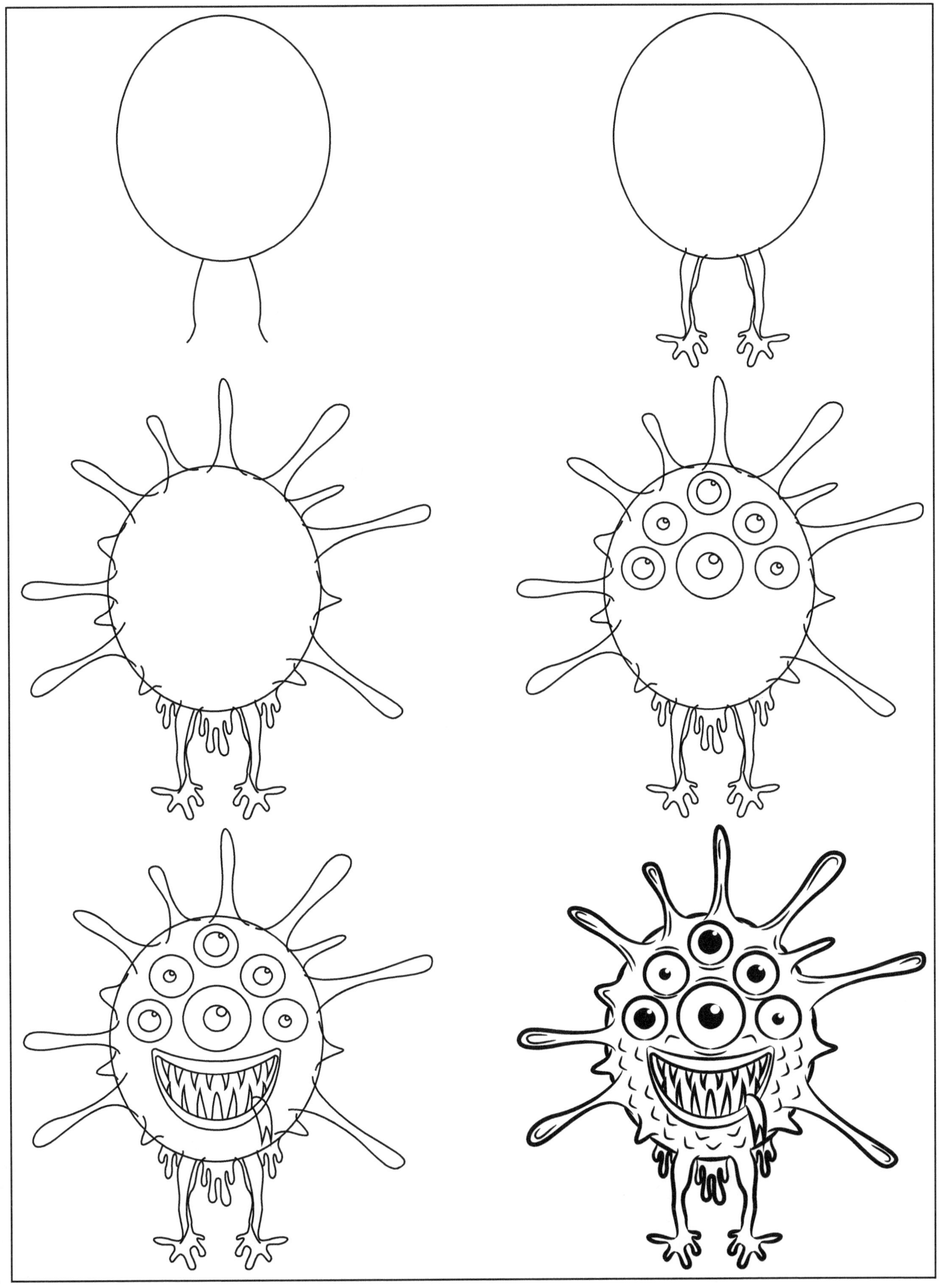

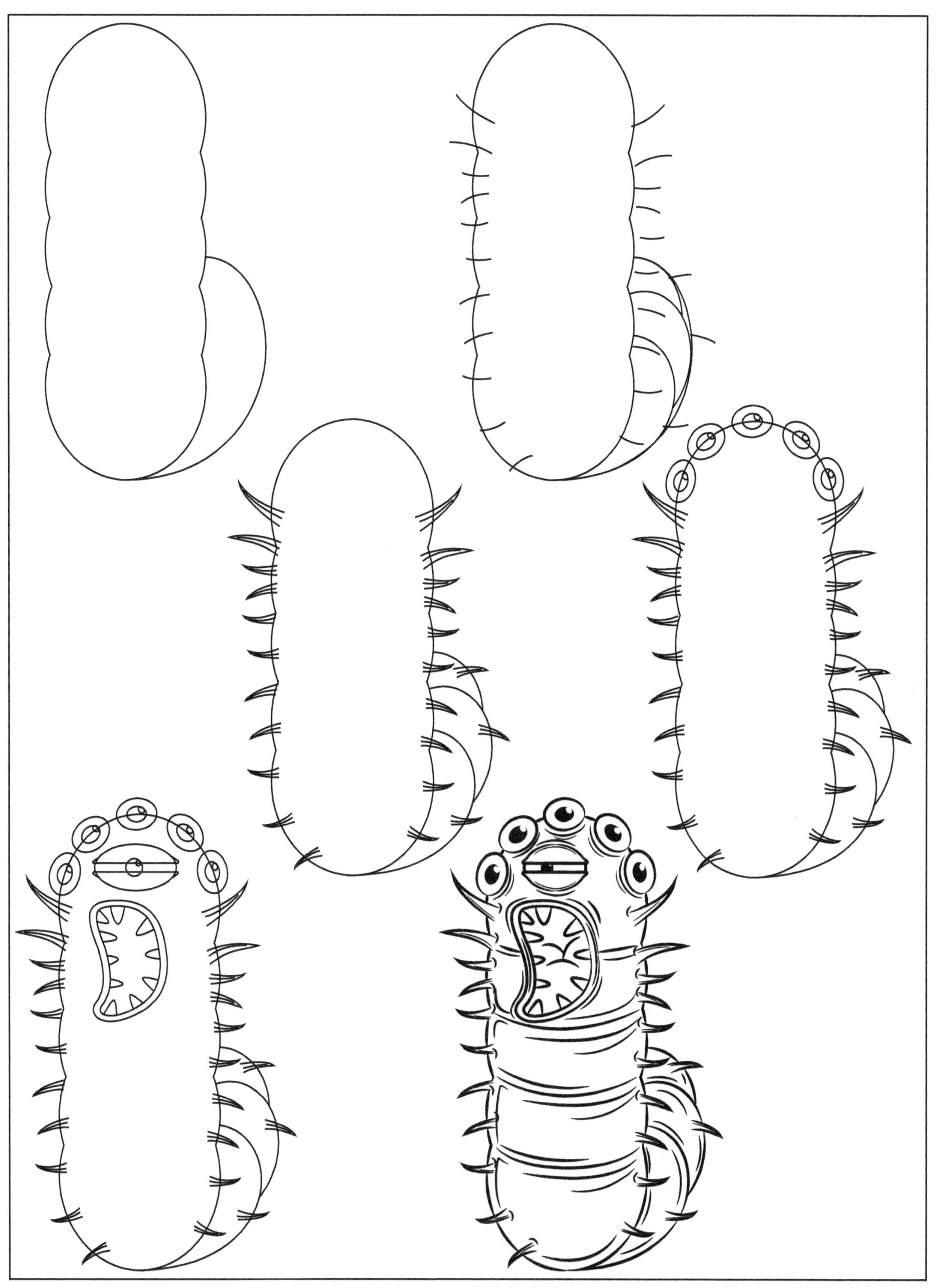

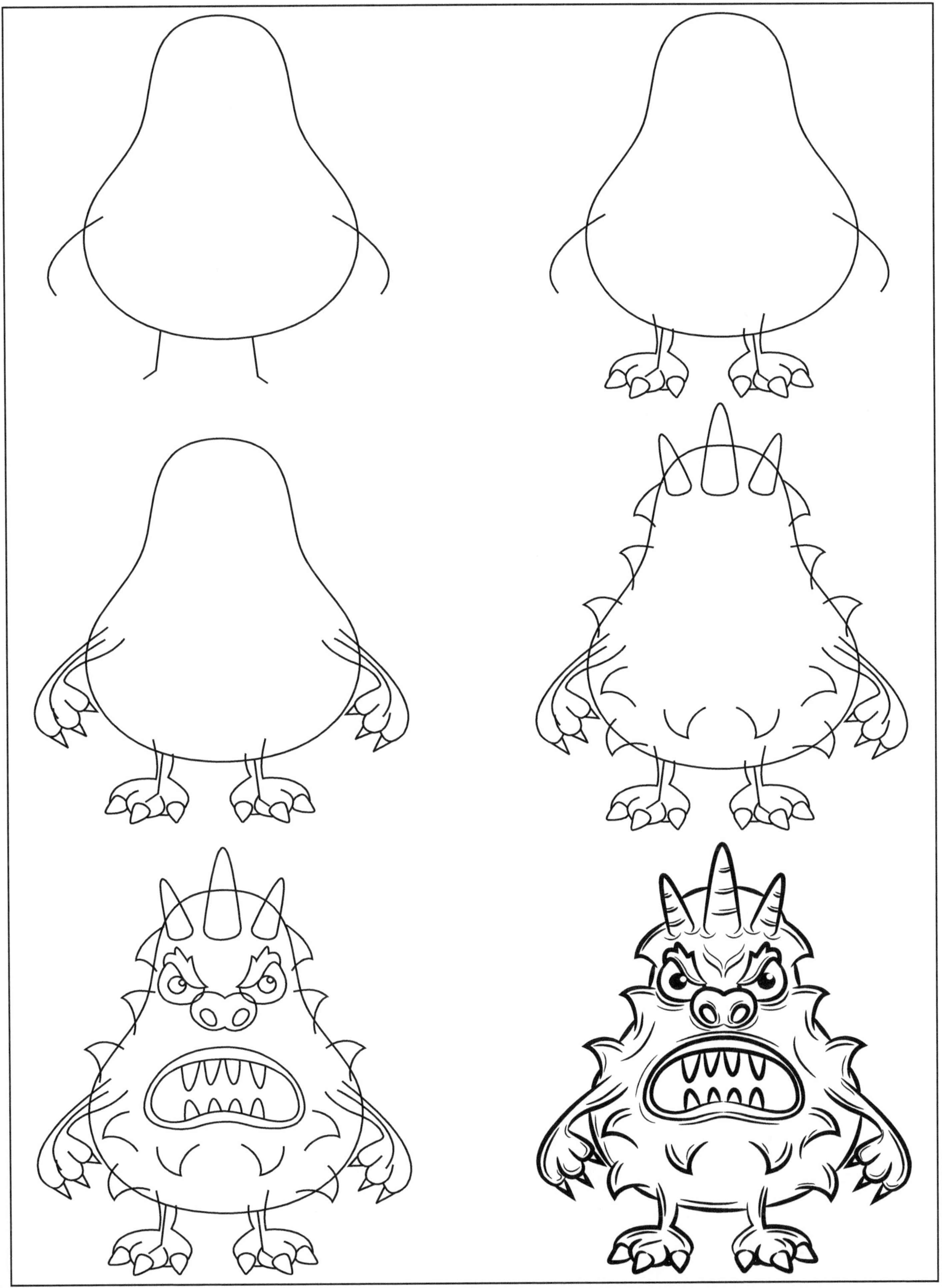

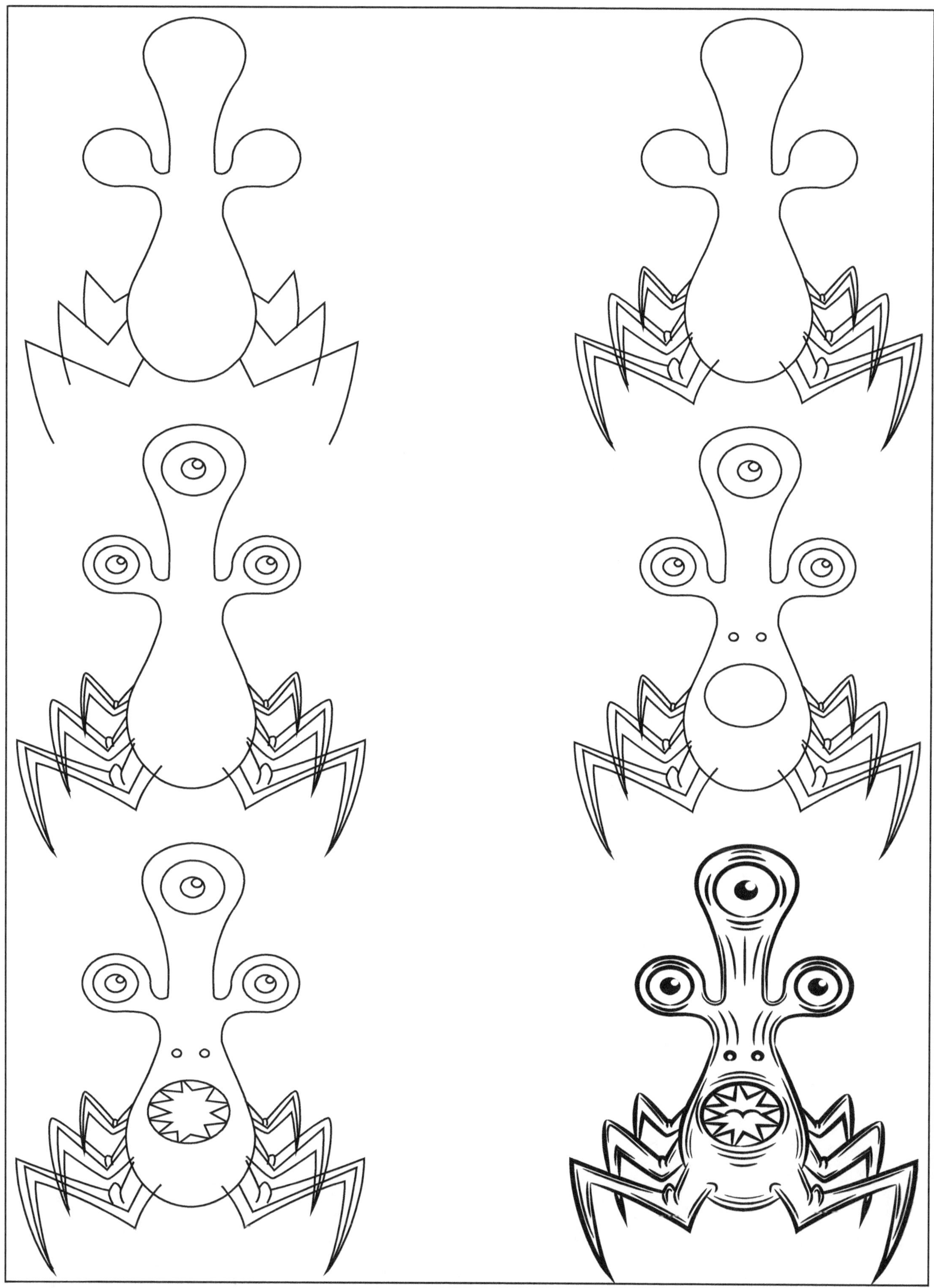

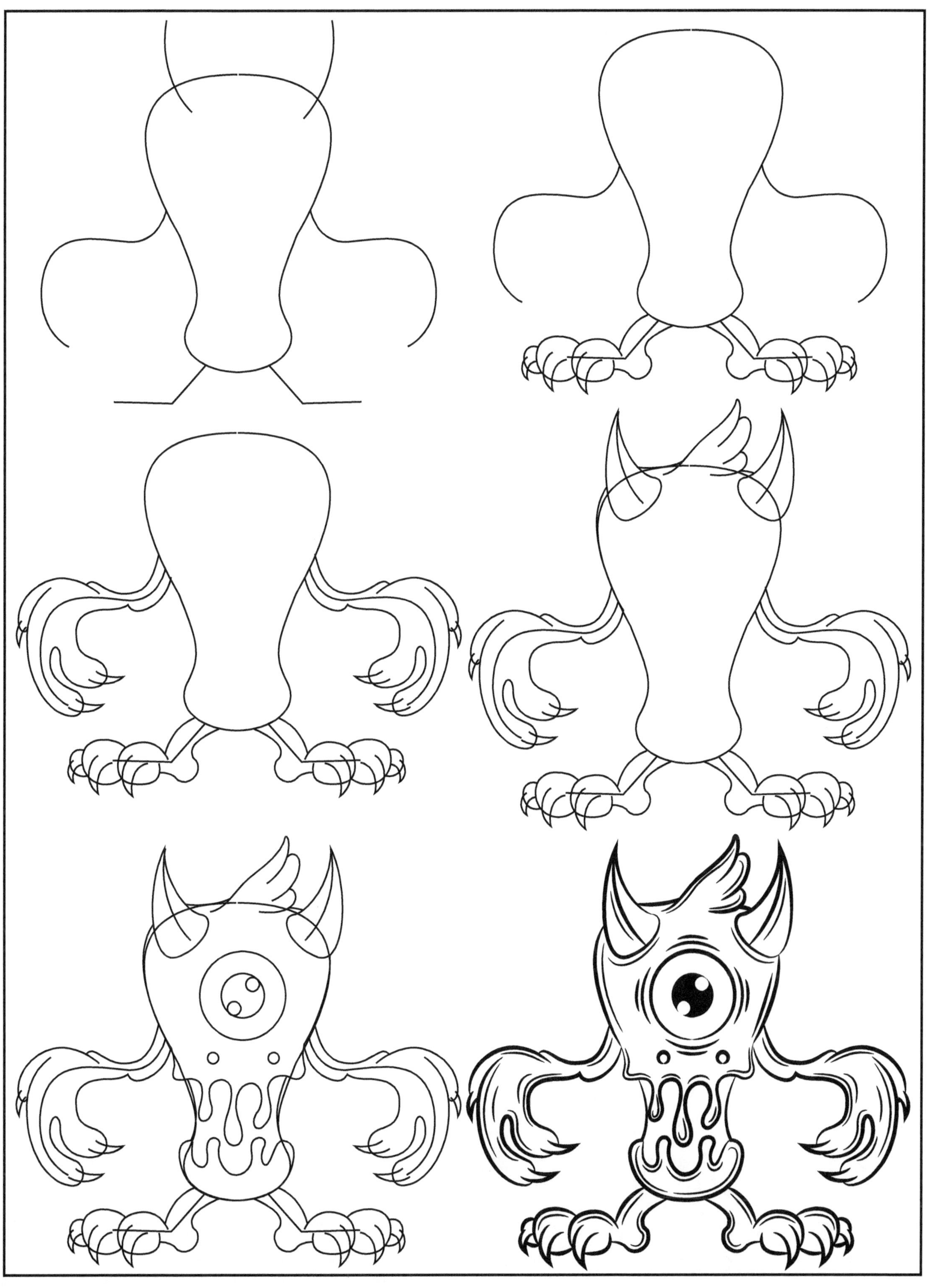

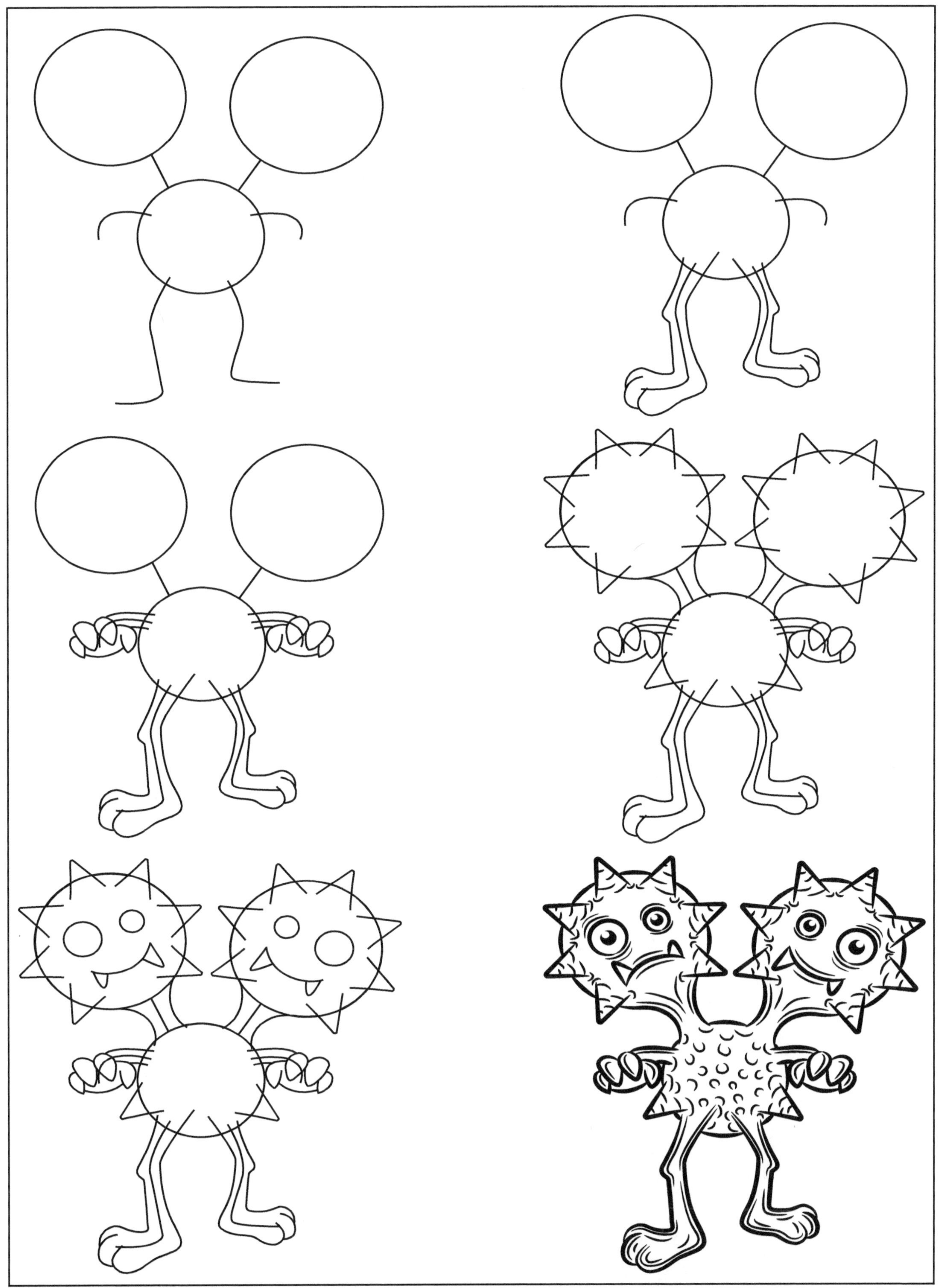

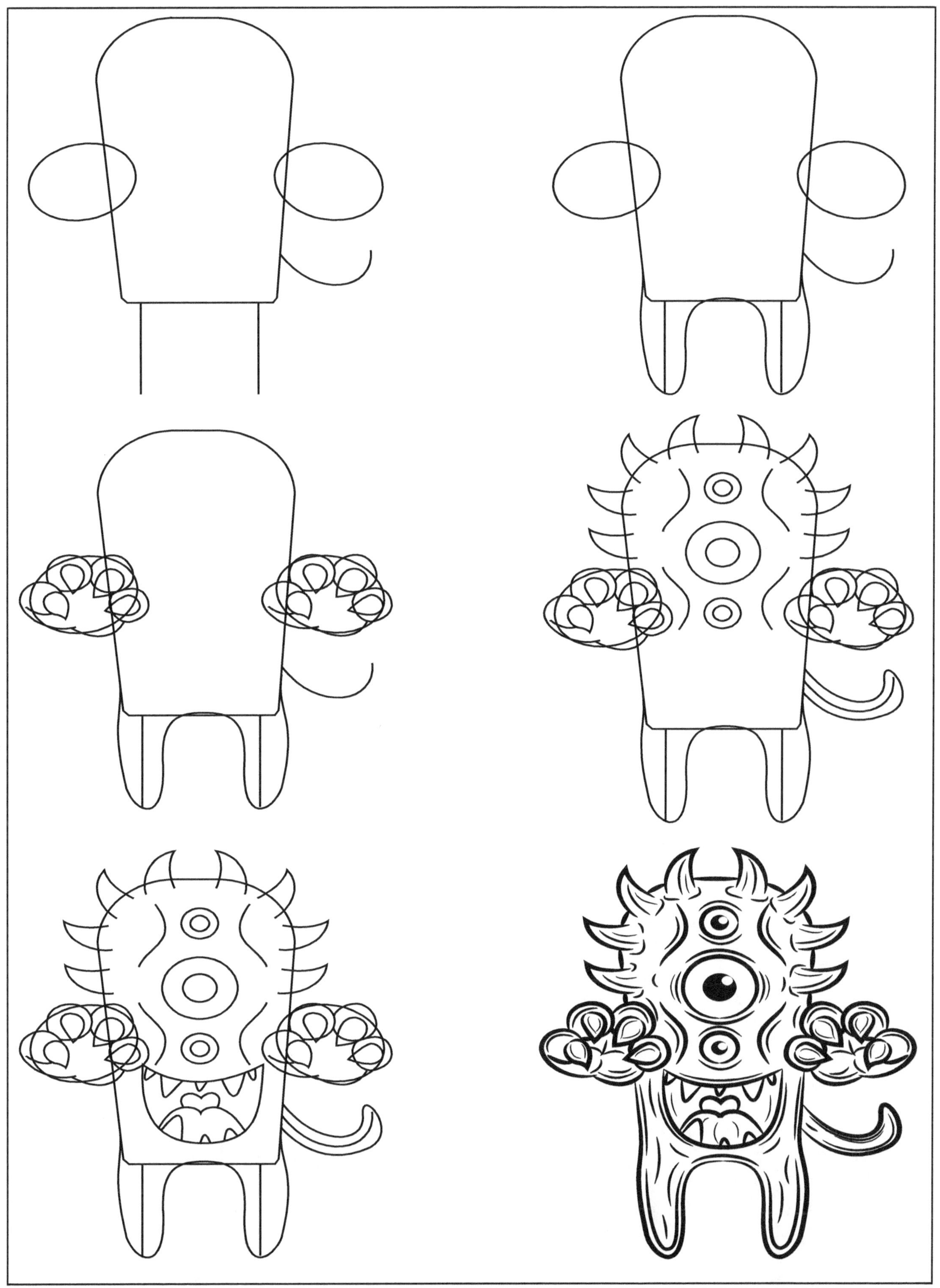

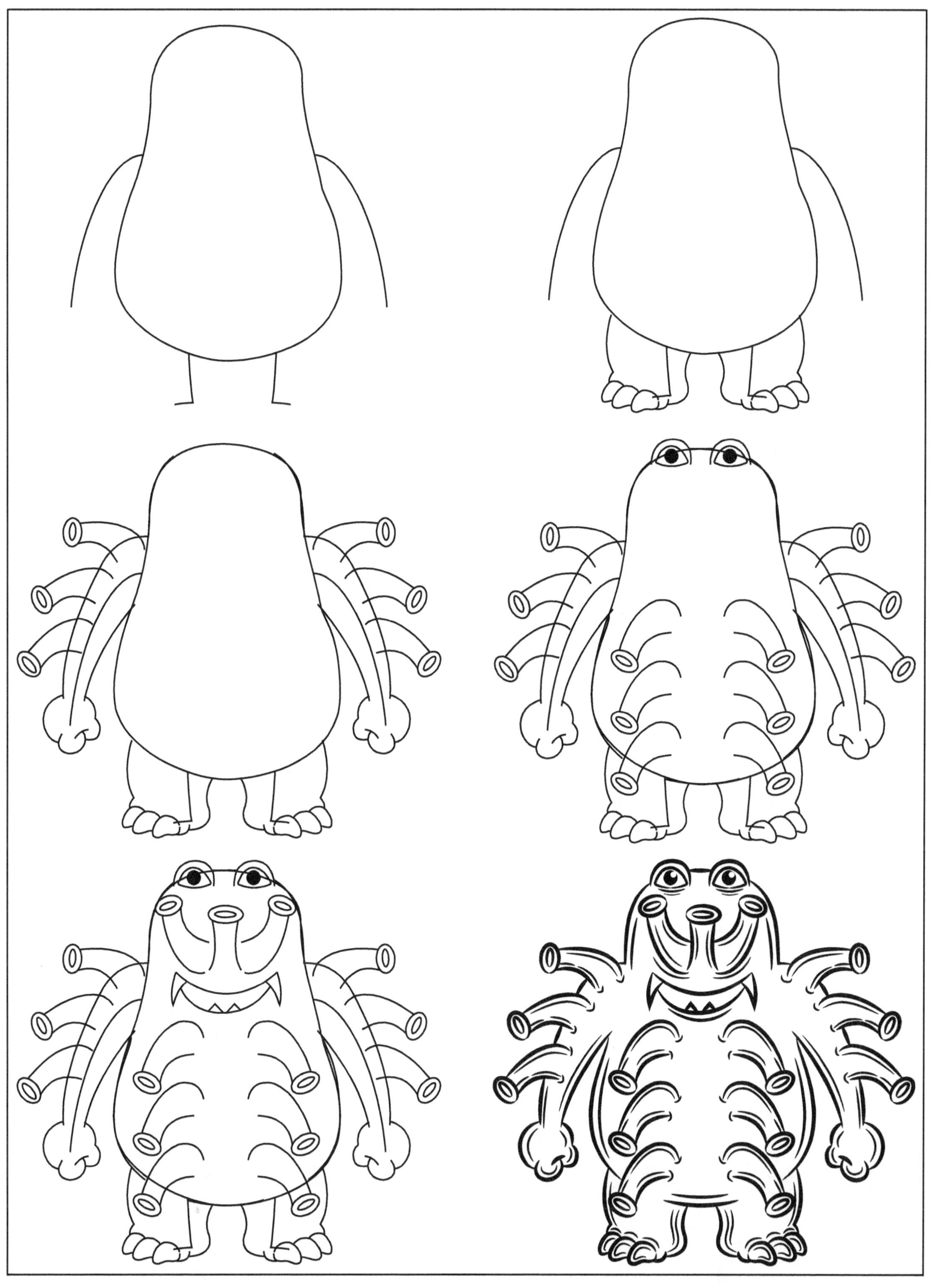